BEST BUCKET FILLER EVER!

God's Plan
for Your Happiness

By Carol McCloud

Illustrated by Glenn Zimmer

Bucket Fillosophy®

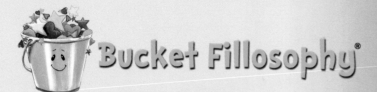

BUCKET FILLOSOPHY® is an imprint of Bucket Fillers, Inc.
PO Box 255, Brighton, MI 48116 • (810) 229-5468

bucketfillers101.com

Author's Acknowledgments

In the 1960s, Dr. Donald O. Clifton (1924-2003) first created
the "Dipper and Bucket" story that has now been passed along
for decades. Dr. Clifton later went on to co-author the #1 *New York Times*
bestseller *How Full is Your Bucket?* and was named the Father of Strengths
Psychology.

A portion of the proceeds from this book is being donated
to fill the buckets of children and families.

Illustrated and designed by Glenn Zimmer.
Edited by Caryn Butzke and Sandy Richardson.

Library of Congress Cataloging-in-Publication Data

Names: McCloud, Carol. | Zimmer, Glenn, illustrator.
Title: Best bucket filler ever! God's plan for your happiness / by Carol McCloud ;
    illustrated by Glenn Zimmer.
Description: Brighton, MI : Bucket Fillosophy, 2020. |
    Based on the ever-popular bucketfilling book series, readers will
    experience God in a new way — as their best bucket filler ever!
Identifiers: LCCN 2019912838 (print) | ISBN 9781945369193 (paperback) |
    ISBN 9781945369216 (e-books)
Subjects: BISAC: JUVENILE NONFICTION / Social Topics / Values & Virtues. |
    JUVENILE NONFICTION / Social Topics / Emotions & Feelings.
LC record available at https://lccn.loc.gov/2019912838
Printed in the United States on recycled paper.

10 9 8 7 6 5 4 3 2 1

From the beginning of time,
God created everything.

God created the heavens and the earth.

Day and night.

Water and land.

Plants and trees.

The sun, moon, and stars.

All fish, birds, and animals . . . every living thing.

God created every person who
ever lived, and God created you.
Every single person is loved by God.

Before you were born,
God breathed into a small, invisible
bucket that was made a part of you
and filled it with love and light.
God was your first "bucket filler"
and you were happy.

Every day and everywhere, in many ways,
God fills buckets with love and light.

God wants every bucket filled and every person happy.

God created you
to be a bucket filler too,
someone who treats
everyone with love
and kindness.

You can fill buckets
because God first
filled yours.

God's plan is perfect.
You will sleep peacefully because . . .
the happiness you give to others, God gives
back to you. Everyone's bucket is filled.

Filling buckets is like planting seeds in a garden.
God grows each seed you plant.

The tiny seeds of love and kindness you plant
will blossom into a harvest of happiness
for you and many others.

God also wants you to fill your own bucket — to make friends, work together, rest, play, laugh, learn, and love.

God wants you to discover and enjoy your God-given talents and the wonderful world created for you.

Bird Seed

God never forces you to be a bucket filler. You are not a puppet. God allows you to choose what you say and do. You can be kind and fill a bucket with happiness or . . .

You can be unkind and dip into a bucket and take away some happiness.

God knows how easy it can be to dip into a bucket
and remove some happiness when you're upset
or only thinking about yourself.

God understands and forgives more than anyone.
God only asks you to think about what you've done,
admit when you've done wrong, and try to do better.

Because God is always with you, you can talk to God anytime and anywhere about anything. You can thank God, say you're sorry, or ask God for help.

God always hears, cares, and wants the best for you.
God loves you.

God loves everyone.
Many people don't know God
loves them, and there is an
emptiness in their buckets.

Many people feel lonely and sad because they don't know how special they are or how to fill buckets.

What if people everywhere knew how much God loved them and that they were created in God's image to be bucket fillers?

What if everyone learned to fill buckets?

People everywhere would be happy. They would learn to love God, love others, and love themselves. They would do their best to treat everyone with the same kindness and respect they would like to receive.

People everywhere would use their time and talents to fill buckets. They would look for ways to help and do good, and fill their own buckets, too.

GET WELL!

People everywhere would work together to create a circle of love, light, peace, joy, friendship, and kindness that includes everyone.

People everywhere would know who
to thank when they see a meadow
of flowers, a glowing sunset, a
starlit sky, or other beauty.
God the Creator is filling
their buckets.

And, as you follow God's plan, you will travel merrily on the road of happiness lined with all the buckets you fill. That's because . . .

God is your best bucket filler ever, and you are a bucket filler, too!

About the Author

Carol McCloud, the "Bucket Lady," is the author of ten books, which began with the ever-popular *Have You Filled a Bucket Today? A Guide to Daily Happiness for Kids* in 2006. By trade, Carol is a speaker, author, and certified emotional intelligence trainer. Her books have sold three million copies and have been translated into many different languages. A champion for bucket filling, Carol works with a powerful presenter team who strive to help people of all ages and occupations lead happier lives by growing in kindness, self-control, resilience, and forgiveness. For more information, visit **bucketfillers101.com**.

About the Illustrator

Glenn Zimmer's passion for art started at a very young age. He spent his formative years drawing and making his own humor magazines and comic books. Upon graduation from the Art Institute of Philadelphia, he began working in graphic design and illustration in the retail and publication markets, eventually becoming a seasoned art director and editorial illustrator. In 2013, he began creatively and lovingly illustrating and designing bucketfilling books. Glenn has served on the faculty of the Pennsylvania College of Art & Design, Cabrini University, and Moore College of Art & Design. For more information, visit **gzimmer.myportfolio.com**.

Dedications

For Pastors Jean and Bill Tulip, who showed me what God's love looked like. — CM

For my mother, Phyllis Marie Zimmer, the first person to teach me the power of love and kindness. — GZ